WASHINGTON, D.C.

GALLERY BOOKS
An Imprint of W. H. Smith Publishers Inc.
112 Madison Avenue
New York City 10016

This edition first published in U.S.
in 1990 by Gallery Books,
an imprint of W.H. Smith Publishers, Inc.
112 Madison Avenue, New York, New York 10016

ISBN 0-8317-8838-0

Printed and bound in Spain

For rights information about the photographs in
this book please contact:

The Image Bank
111 Fifth Avenue, New York, NY 10003

Producer: Solomon M. Skolnick
Author: Nancy Millichap Davies
Design Concept: Lesley Ehlers
Designer: Ann-Louise Lipman
Editor: Terri L. Hardin
Production: Valerie Zars
Photo Researcher: Edward Douglas
Assistant Photo Researcher: Robert V. Hale
Editorial Assistant: Carol Raguso

Title page: *The Washington
Monument from Signers' Memorial
in Constitution Gardens on the Mall,
where stones honor the 56 signers of
the Declaration of Independence.*
Opposite: *The Capitol dome, symbol
of Federal government, rises 285 feet
above its hilltop site.*

The District of Columbia began as an idea. Congress voted in 1790 to establish a location for the national government newly defined by the Constitution. All American cities up to that time had evolved—Washington was legislated into being. The senators and representatives gathered in the first Congresses, each representing one of a collection of jealous British colonies newly welded into a nation, and hotly debated the location of the proposed capital as they moved like nomads from city to city: New York, Princeton, Philadelphia. Eventually they agreed that the permanent capital of their new republican democracy should be on a site not located in any former colony.

George Washington, a Virginia planter as well as a victorious Revolutionary general, picked out the tract of land that would eventually bear his name. What he chose as "the Federal City" was a hundred square miles of Maryland and Virginia countryside, including the two small river ports of Georgetown and Alexandria. The site was attractive to wealthy planters who had considerable political power in that early Congress, as well as to President Washington, who lived only a day's ride from the capital-to-be.

Like the capitals of many of the original states, it was located at the upper limit of river navigation and was therefore a natural center for trade and transport.

In this vista eastward across the Potomac, a succession of monuments— Marine Corps Memorial, Lincoln Memorial, Washington Monument— leads to the Capitol.

The semicircular South Portico of the White House, supported by Ionic columns. Below: For many citizens, the President's house is as much a symbol of the highest office in the land as is the official Presidential seal. Opposite: The White House's South Lawn. Eighteen acres of parkland surround the symmetrical, dignified Palladian structure designed by James Hoban in 1792.

The state of Maryland contributed 69 square miles and Virginia 31 square miles to make up the diamond-shaped tract, most of it still forested, that lay at the junction of the Potomac and Anacostia Rivers. (In 1846, Alexandria residents successfully petitioned Congress to retrocede the Virginia land to the original state so today Washington consists of the 69 square miles which were formerly part of the state of Maryland.)

Pierre L'Enfant, a French engineer who had accompanied the Marquis de Lafayette when that young nobleman came to aid the American colonists in their rebellion against Britain, created the spacious urban layout of the Washington we know today. In 1791, with the Revolutionary War successfully ended and the new Constitution adopted, Major L'Enfant begged George Washington to commission him to design the general outline of the new capital city. Once the first President had agreed, L'Enfant examined the lay of the land, studied a preliminary drawing by Thomas Jefferson and maps of a dozen European cities, and then drew up his detailed map. Unlike the cities which had grown up elsewhere in Britain's North American colonies, his expansive plan of broad avenues and long vistas was modeled along Continental lines.

L'Enfant laid out the city around three principal sites. For the first of these, which he called "Congress House," he selected Jenkins Hill, the highest rise of land in the bowl-shaped tract along the Potomac. The second of

Guests invited to White House events, such as state dinners, pass beneath the two-story porch of the North Portico.

Top, left to right: *Statues in Lafayette Square, just north of the White House. The Marquis de Lafayette. Baron von Steuben, Revolutionary drillmaster and General Washington's aide. Lafayette's friend and fellow supporter of the Revolution, Comte de Rochambeau.* Below: *Andrew Jackson, seventh President.* Opposite: *Departing White House visitors snap photos at the North Door. Tours of the mansion's public rooms are offered five mornings a week.*

these sites, which he reserved fo the "President's House" also stoo on high ground, offering a long view of the Potomac (a view long since blocked by other buildings. Stretching west from his Congres House toward the Potomac, L'Enfant planned a "Grand Avenue" of majestic width, which is today's Mall. It was to end at the third of L'Enfant's principal sites, a monument which he thought would be a statue of George Washington on horse-back, on another rise in the valley landscape near what was then the bank of the Potomac.

The rest of the L'Enfant plan was made up of a regular grid of streets with a foresighted inno-vation: diagonal avenues named for the original states crisscrosse the grid. These 160-foot-wide avenues would not only open vistas throughout the cityscape he envisioned but would also allow quick access from the outskirts of the city into its heart. Seen as impossibly wide in the eighteenth century, they are perfectly adapted to the demands of modern traffic.

The farsighted French engineer worked for the District Commissioners for only a year. He clashed with wealthy local landowners who found that his plan interfered with developmen of their own properties and they convinced Washington to remove him. In the capital's early years

Top to bottom: *A fife and drum corp performs on the South Lawn of the White House. At the Cabinet Room's mahogany table, the President confer with senior staff. Visitors' Entrance at the East Gate.* Opposite: *Inspiring landmarks in an expanse of green, the Washington Monument and the Jefferson Memorial punctuate the view from the White House's South Portico.*

Japanese cherry trees, a gift to the United States Government from the city of Tokyo in 1912, bloom along the Tidal Basin, southwest of the Washington Monument. Thousands come to enjoy their beauty during the early April Cherry Blossom Festival. Opposite: *Above the cherry blossoms, the marble obelisk of the Washington Monument. By law, no other building in the city may approach its 555-foot height.*

he could be seen wandering the dusty or muddy new streets with his dog, gazing upon the development of the city that remained a raw and sprawling place during his lifetime, with a few ambitiou buildings in an alternately dust and swampy bottomland.

At the time, L'Enfant's design seemed so ambitious as to be ridiculous. In the two centuries since, however, L'Enfant's concep tion has in large part supplied th city's master plan. Indeed, only in this century has the plan begu to be fully realized and L'Enfant inspired vision recognized.

A circle of 50 flags rings the base of the Washington Monument. Left: The Constitution Avenue monumen of the U.S. Army Second Division. Opposite: The Second Division Memorial, with its 18-foot-tall gilded bronze sword and marble wings, commemorates 17,669 casualties in two world wars and Korea.

Preceding page: *Time-lapse photography turns Fourth of July fireworks to spangles and streaks on the sky above the Mall and Washington Monument.* This page: *Aglow with sunset rays and floodlight, the Washington Monument seems to rise from the Lincoln Memorial to its west.*

No one is certain about the origin of the name now used for the first building erected in the new capital: was "White House" derived from the gleam of the sandstone facings, from the white paint upon them, or from the Southern custom of referring to the owner's house on a plantation in that way? The design of Irish-American James Hoban, it resembles country houses of the same era built in Ireland for the dominant English aristocracy.

When the federal government occupied the new city in 1800, the White House was by no means complete, but President and Mrs. Adams moved into what there was of it. Construction was still in progress when invading British troops burned down the unfinished structure—along with most of the capital's other public buildings—in 1814. Hoban spent three years rebuilding before President Monroe occupied the mansion, which at that date looked much as it does now. Today's White House however, is almost entirely a reconstruction. The Army Corps of Engineers gutted the tottering original in 1949–1952 and constructed a new interior and foundation on steel piers while President Truman and his family lived across the street.

Jenkins Hill, the highest spot in the Federal City site, had struck Pierre L'Enfant as "a pedestal waiting for a monument." He chose it as the site for the "Congress House." Since then, Capitol Hill has taken on the name of its monument, and the structure that crowns it today represents a considerable evolution from the original building on the site. The District Commissioners held a

The Lincoln Memorial columns and their shadows create a geometric frame for the Washington Monument and its image in the Reflecting Pool.

competition for the best design for the Capitol. Amateur architect Dr. William Thornton's winning entry included a dome, but a far lower and more modest one than the magnificent ornament which tops the building today. Thornton building was completed enough for Congress to meet there in November 1800, when it first convened in the Federal City, but much of the effort of 20 years of construction went up in flames during the British invasion of 1814. Five years later Congress was meeting in a second structure, built upon the ruins.

By the middle of the nineteenth century, as territories became new states and the numbers of senators and representatives multiplied accordingly, the size of the Capitol became inadequate. Congress voted to expand it. At least in part to provide the nearby South with clear evidence of Lincoln's determination to preserve and perpetuate the Union, work on the addition continued during the early years of the Civil War. Spacious chambers were added to house not only the Senate and the House of Representatives, but also the Supreme Court (the Court moved to its own building in 1935.) An elaborately ornamented dome of cast iron, painted white to blend with the building's marble walls, effectively balanced the expanded wings. The revamped Capitol was dedicated in 1863 and had, by and large, the same appearance we know today.

Erected in 1922 in the form of a Greek temple, the Lincoln Memorial lies at the western end of an axis running from the Capitol along the Mall. Below: The Reflecting Pool stretches from the Memorial's circular lawn toward the Washington Monument.

Top, left to right: *In his 19-foot-high marble sculpture of Lincoln, Daniel Chester French portrayed a President wearied by the cares of war. Bathed by setting sun, the massive figure faces east toward the Capitol. US Army personnel supply the Memorial's honor guard.*

Atop the dome was a figure known to some as "Freedom" and others as "Armed Freedom." Freedom's headgear, originally a Phrygian or liberty cap, was changed to a crested helmet at the insistence of Jefferson Davis, secretary of war in Lincoln's first cabinet, who feared such a symbol would encourage abolitionists and would-be runaway slaves.

L'Enfant's original plan for the Federal City provided for a "Washington statue" at the approximate spot where the Washington Monument now stands. The sort of memorial which would best commemorate the nation's first President was debated for decades. When the Continental Congress voted for a memorial in 1783, its members had an equestrian statue in mind. Robert Mills' design, winner of a competition 50 years later, included not only a 700-foot obelisk but also a circular Greek temple around the base. The cornerstone of the monument was laid in 1848, but because of funding problems and interruption by the Civil War, the tower stood uncompleted for many years. Mills' design was further refined after the Civil War by George Marsh, a U.S. ambassador to Italy, who made a study of ancient obelisks in Europe and Egypt and recommended important changes and simplifications,

Preceding page: West of the Lincoln Memorial, the Potomac River reflects its floodlit peristyle and bursts of Independence Day fireworks on the Mall. This page, top to bottom: The Jefferson Memorial shares the Tidal Basin's shores with Japanese cherry trees. The 1943 Memorial, a rotunda beneath a low dome, recalls Monticello, the home Jefferson designed for himself. Within, a 19-foot bronze statue of the third President faces the White House.

including the idea that the monument's height should be reduced to 10 times its baseline, or a bit more than 555 feet. Army engineers took over the construction, and the capstone with its cast-aluminum tip was finally placed on the world's tallest masonry structure in 1884. Visible for many miles outside the city, with red lights flashing a warning to aircraft by night in the windows at the base of the pyramidal cap, it remains the District's most conspicuous structure and a distinctive memorial to the patriot and leader who gave the city its name.

If Washington—the man—was indeed first in war and first in peace, it must be argued that wise, folksy, martyred Abraham Lincoln, popularly viewed as the Savior of the Union, has usurped the position of being first in the hearts of his countrymen. The move to erect a memorial to the 16th President began within a few years of his assassination in 1865.

Some saw the appointed site, a wetland at the time, as unpromising. Speaker of the House Joseph Cannon was heard to declare that he would not permit the building of a memorial to Abraham Lincoln in "that g-d-swamp." But the swamp was drained, and an 80-foot-high marble temple to Lincoln's memory, modeled on the Parthenon in Athens and housing a monumental statue, was dedicated in 1922. In one of the great ironies of that age of segregation, a distinguished participant in the memorial's

Visitors are reflected in the long, polished, black granite walls of the Vietnam Veterans Memorial, inscribed with the names of all the war's dead.

Preceding page: *A sculpture of three Vietnam-era servicemen in combat attire complements the memorial's honor roll (top). Among the names of more than 58,000 who died in the conflict, visitors leave their tributes (bottom).* This page: *Icons of political and intellectual life in Washington, the Capitol Dome and a tower of the earliest Smithsonian building rise above the Mall.*

dedication—Afro-American Dr. Robert Moton, president of the Tuskegee Institute—was not permitted to sit on the speakers platform, but had to make his way to the podium from the section across the road reserved for "Negroes" to deliver his dedicatory address.

L'Enfant thought that embassies would line Grand Avenue, now the Mall. Instead, the buildings of the Smithsonia Institution border the broad expanse of open ground which stretches from the Capitol to the Washington Monument. Seed

The original building of the Smithsonian Institution, today known as "the Castle," was the latest in Goth Revival architecture when complete in 1855. Formal Victorian flowerbed reflect the era of construction.

oney to found the institution
as a gift to the United States
om an Englishman who never
t foot in the country. James
mithson (1765–1829), the
legitimate son of the Duke of
orthumberland, lived much of
s life in Europe as a scientist.
is will provided that if his heir,
nephew, should die without an
eir, his estate of $550,000 should
e used to found "a Washingtonian
tablishment for the increase
nd diffusion of knowledge
mong men." Smithson's nephew
d die childless, and the world's
rgest complex of museums is
e result.

*he Hirshhorn Museum (1974),
ntemporary art's home on the Mall,
ntains Auguste Rodin's 1886
ronze group, "The Burghers of
lais," in the sculpture garden.
elow: Abstract sculptures embellish
e Hirshhorn's plaza.*

The Spirit of St. Louis, *in which Charles Lindbergh made the first solo flight across the Atlantic in 1927*. Below: *Examples of historically significant planes hang from the ceiling of the National Air and Space Museum.*

Congress spent a decade debating the use of Smithson's bequest, a huge sum at the time, and finally voted to create an institution which would sponsor scientific investigations and publish the results. The institution's first building, today's Smithsonian Castle, went up on the Mall in the 1850's.

With the Centennial Exposition of 1876, the Smithsonian's mission changed. At the end of this grand international fair, many countries that had sent exhibits to Philadelphia donated them to the U.S. Government, at least partially to avoid the costs of shipping them home. The decision to send 40 train cars of these gifts to the Smithsonian made of it an instant museum, soon to earn its nickname "the nation's attic," and occasioned the building of the National Museum, the present Arts and Industries building. Eight more Smithsonian buildings have joined these Victorian-era structures during the twentieth century. The collections they house range from the inaugural gowns of the nation's First Ladies in the Museum of American History to a stuffed eight-ton African elephant in the Museum of Natural History, to a walk-through model of the Skylab space station in the most popular hall, the Air and Space Museum.

The Mall is a rewarding destination not only for visitors of a scientific and technological

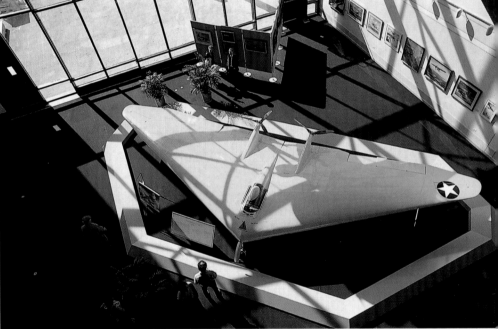

Top to bottom: *At the Smithsonian's Air and Space Museum, rockets, manned spacecraft, and guided missiles compose a popular exhibit in Space Hall. The Northrop N-1M Flying Wing was far ahead of its time in 1940. A NASA jet.*

Preceding page: *A distinctive I. M. Pei design, the National Gallery of Art's East Building (1978) includes offices for curators and administrators as well as gallery space.* This page: *The National Gallery of Art (top) opened in 1941 to house millionaire Andrew Mellon's art collection, a gift to the nation. Glass pyramids (bottom) channel light to the underground passage linking Pei's East Building with the original structure, now called the West Building.*

Daniel Chester French's "Victory" tops a column before the Executive Offices, built in 1888 to house the departments of State, and Navy. Below: The Smithsonian's National Museum of Natural History on the Mall. Opposite: The National Museum of Nat. History (1910) contains over 80 million objects relating to the natural environment and to the development of human beings.

bent, but also for art lovers. The Smithsonian's first organized art collection came in the early 1920's from Detroit industrialist Charles Freer, who also provided the building to house his Asian art objects. The Freer Gallery was joined in 1974 by the concrete doughnut of the Hirshhorn Museum, which holds 12,000 contemporary paintings and sculptures collected and given to the nation by investor Joseph Hirshhorn. The 1980's saw the construction near the Castle of a pair of mostly underground galleries, the Sackler for another wealth of Asian objects and the National Museum of African Art.

Washington's greatest treasury of art, the National Gallery, also stands on the Mall part of the Smithsonian but administered by a separate board of directors. The National Gallery began in 1936 with a gift of 126 paintings from industrialist and former Treasury Secretary Andrew Mellon. Mr. Mellon also paid for the space in which to display his bequest and the other gifts of art that he correctly assumed would follow.

The classical marble structure of 100 galleries was completed in 1941. By the 1960's increases in the collection and in popular enthusiasm for art made more space necessary. Thanks to the generosity of Andrew Mellon's son Paul, a very different yet

The Capitol's vast dome balances the spreading wings where the House and the Senate meet. Left: *Within the eye of the 180-foot-high dome, Italian artist Constantino Brumidi painted* "The Apotheosis of Washington" in *fresco in 1865.* Opposite: *Inauguration Day bunting drapes the Capitol's façade. Presidents are traditionally inaugurated on its steps.*

Grand stairways and porticos of double columns lead to the House of Representatives (top) and the Senate Chamber (opposite).

Preceding page: *On the rim of the Reflecting Pool, an equestrian statue of Ulysses S. Grant makes a dramatic silhouette against the Capitol's west front.* This page: *The Capitol's massive dome, here reflecting sunset light, is made of cast iron, painted white, and topped with a 19-foot-high statue of Freedom.*

Two rows of Corinthian columns support the pediment of the marble *Supreme Court Building (1935)*. Below: *The Library of Congress, established within the Capitol for congressmen's research use in 1800, now serves as a national library of over 80 million volumes.* Opposite: *Main Reading Room, Library of Congress (1897)*. *Its ornate dome, 160 feet high, arches over banks of catalogues and tiers of mahogany desks.*

complementary structure, in the same pink Tennessee marble as the original, rose across the street. A broad underground corridor housing cafés and bookshops joins the East Building to its neighbor.

The official Washington which has evolved from L'Enfant design over the past two centuries, the Washington of grand green spaces and national monuments and museums, is a city of outsiders. There are the visitors who come for a day or weekend or week of sightseeing and, perhaps, of paying their respects to those who have died in the nation's service at the Lincoln Memorial or the Vietnam Veterans' Memorial, or across the Potomac in Arlington National Cemetery. There are others, also outsiders, who stay in Washington for a period of years because they have been elected or appointed to carry on the business of this government, or sent as diplomats by other governments. They often live in Georgetown, west of downtown Washington proper, where the business of government goes on unofficially after hours in elegantly renovated town houses and restaurants featuring international cuisines.

Top to bottom: *Triumphant renovations. The 1899 Old Post Office with its 315-foot Romanesque tower (top) and central court (bottom) now houses the National Endowment for the Humanities as well as chic shops and restaurants. Spacious Union Station (center) still serves rail passengers, but doubles as an elegant shopping mall.*

Top, left to right: *Grand entrances. National Archives Building, storehouse of government records. Statue of Alexander Hamilton, first Secretary of the Treasury, before the Treasury Building. Marble walkway to the Federal Reserve Building.* Below: *The concave east façade of the Federal Building.*

Preceding pages, left: *Amid modern mosaics, worshippers at Mass face the marble-canopied high altar of the Roman Catholic Shrine of the Sacred Heart.* Preceding pages, right: *The Episcopal Cathedral Church of St. Peter and St. Paul, also called the National Cathedral, was begun in 1907 in fourteenth-century English Gothic style.* This page: *A bronze head of John Kennedy dominates the foyer of his official Washington memorial.* Below: *The Kennedy Center for the Performing Arts opened in 1971. It contains three theatres, an opera house, a concert hall, and a performing arts library.*

Its location on the Potomac makes the Kennedy Center convenient for out-of-towners coming in over the city's western bridges to attend performances.

*The oldest U. S. Catholic college, Georgetown University was founded in
1789 by the nation's first bishop, John Carroll of Baltimore, who opened his
academy to students of "every Religious Profession." Below: Construction
began in 1792 on Georgetown University's first building, Old North.*

An additional and larger
population of men and women,
many of whose families have
lived here for generations, are
more permanent residents.
Throughout the city's history,
the percentage of African-
Americans in Washington's
population has steadily increased,
making up more than 70% of the
population today.

Unlike most other U.S.
citizens, Washingtonians do not
enjoy the privilege of represen-
tation in Congress. Immediately

After the Civil War, much progress was made toward giving the people of the District—about 30% of whom were African-American at that time—control over their own affairs. However, the backlash that followed the reforms of the Reconstruction era and the increasing trend toward segregation soon erased those gains. By 1874, a more conservative Congress had reinstated the system of district commissioners appointed by the President.

The civil rights movements that began in the mid-twentieth century brought the issue of home rule back to public debate.

Modest and charming town houses evoke an earlier time in Georgetown. Below: Barge rides on the Chesapeake and Ohio Canal. Georgetown was already a thriving river port when Congress located the Federal City to its east.

In 1970, Congress decreed that Washingtonians might elect a nonvoting delegate to Congress, and in 1975 the citizens elected a mayor, Walter Washington, an a 13-member city council. Today, the idea of giving statehood to the District is extremely popular with a majority of its citizens. Whether the Congress is ready to consider statehood for the District in which it sits remains an open question. For now, L'Enfant's and Washington's Federal City remains, as it was at its founding, a region set apart – a District which exists first and foremost for the administration of all the rest of the nation.

The Marine Corps Memorial in Arlington National Cemetery commemorates a heroic moment in World War II. Below: *The Pentagon Building is home to the Department of Defense.* Opposite: *The pose of the figures in the Marine Corps Memorial recalls the inspiration, Joe Rosenthal's photograph of Marines raising the flag on Iwo Jima Island.*

Both the famous and the unknown lie in honored repose at Arlington National Cemetery, the largest burial ground for those who served in the nation's armed forces. Below: An honor guard accompanies the horse-drawn caisson in this Marine Corps funeral procession.

A guard marches before the Tomb of the Unknowns. Remains of unidentified servicemen from each of the nation's wars in the twentieth century lie here. Below: On Veterans' Day, services at the adjacent Memorial Amphitheatre honor these and others who died serving the nation.

President John F. Kennedy's words, inscribed at his gravesite, reflect the sacrifice he and others buried in Arlington made for the nation and for freedom. Opposite: An Eternal Flame was lit at his funeral, and flowers from those who mourn him adorn Kennedy's simple grave. Following pages: Night view across the Potomac from Arlington: illuminated monuments and fountains define the urban landscape. As seen from Arlington, the downtown panorama in floodlight and Fourth of July fireworks.

Index of Photography

All photographs courtesy of The Image Bank,
except where indicated *.